Practic
SMALL
GARDENING

Ian Murray

The Crowood Press

First published in 1995 by
The Crowood Press Ltd
Ramsbury, Marlborough
Wiltshire SN8 2HR

British Library Cataloguing-in-Publication Data

A catalogue record for this book is available from the British
Library.

ISBN 1 85223 869 0

Dedication

To my Kathy, a big inspiration in a small garden

Picture Credits
Line-drawings by Claire Upsdale-Jones
All photographs are by the author except for those on pages 1;
2–3; 4; 10 (top); 13 (left); 18; 23 (both); 28; 30 (right); 31; 32
(both); 34; 35; 37 (all); 38; 40; 44; 47; 58 and 59 which are by
Sue Atkinson; those on pages 9; 10 (bottom); 13 (right); 22 and
33 which are by Yvonne Rees; those on page 54 which are by
D. Pike; that on page 39 which is by Brynphotos; and that on
page 55 which is by S. Wooster.

Typeset in Optima by Chippendale Type Ltd,
Otley, West Yorkshire
Printed and bound by Paramount Printing Group, Hong Kong
Colour Separation by Next Graphic Limited, Hong Kong.

CONTENTS

INTRODUCTION

After the Romans introduced gardens into Britain, there followed centuries of social and cultural turmoil which resulted in most of the population having to work on the land and only a wealthy minority with leisure gardens. In the last hundred years, a peaceful revolution has brought the opportunity for everyone to cultivate plants, and nowadays the ownership of a garden is the norm rather than the exception.

The size of gardens has varied enormously through the ages and all would agree that the country estates of the aristocracy and those of the rich industrialists were certainly large. Some gardens are still measured in acres but the vast majority are much smaller; it poses the question, what is a small garden? Such a description could be applied to a six-inch pot, a window-box and the plot attached to a semi-detached house in Milton Keynes. This book carefully avoids confronting the issue, relying on owners to decide on their own definition in a world of changing comparatives.

Fortunately, the actual dimensions are unimportant. What one must realize is that the smaller the area of cultivation, the more important is plant selection and an efficient garden design. Each plant should justify its inclusion in the plan by providing beauty and, preferably, long-term performance. Every piece of the plot should offer interest and delight for as much of the year as is possible. That is the philosophy of small-garden cultivation and I sincerely hope that this book will help to achieve an attractive environment and stimulate an absorbing leisure activity.

A small pool surrounded by rockery brightens up the smallest gardens.

1 • SMALL BEGINNINGS

The prospect of undertaking a new gardening project can be exciting in the extreme and certain times of the year provide additional stimulus. Sometimes the urge to get started overcomes the sensible requirement for a plan and some people may simply wish to pick up a spade and immerse themselves in frantic endeavour, confident that inspiration will guide their hand. The reality of this scenario is usually confusion and error resulting in the need for considerable correction work. The better option is to spend an hour or two in the garden with tape-measure and notebook and when an acceptable drawing (preferably to scale) has been made, numerous ideas can be given temporary existence in two dimensions. Visualizing to and from plans does require some experience but the actual process of committing thoughts to paper is always instructive.

Next comes the important decision about your intended relationship with the garden and your attitude towards gardening. Even a small garden can be a positive tyrant with the hapless gardener becoming enslaved by ambitions and all the work that needs to be done. Some gardeners relish this but others resent the demands made on them, especially if their other interests are competing for attention. For many, there is huge pleasure in tending plants but for others this is drudgery: the garden's function is after all to provide a pleasant environment with the minimum maintenance. The initial decision may not last so it is wiser to plan for a moderately low level of involvement and to deal with increasing enthusiasm if it arises.

A collection of evergreen plants in a variety of tubs can be usefully deployed throughout the year on all the hard surfaces of the garden.

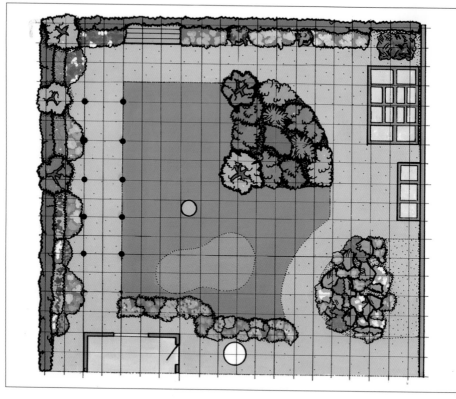

Time spent experimenting with designs on graph paper – before making any final decisions – saves time and expense later.

Assessment

Where the garden is on a newly developed site, there will probably be a rectangular shape, at the front and back, with lawns laid with turf. Otherwise, the space is quite empty and, if you are lucky, cleared of builder's debris both above and below ground level; this presents the opportunity of being responsible for every single element of the final picture.

When the garden is acquired through buying an older house, there will almost certainly be a full complement of plants ranging from trees and shrubs to herbaceous subjects and bulbs. In this case, it is advisable to do nothing until at least one summer has passed so that most of the plants can show their merits and make a plea for inclusion in the garden's future. Notebook and pencil are required again because action is better taken in late autumn or early winter when the plants will be more difficult to identify. If a knowledgeable friend or neighbour is available, the plants can be named and labelled while in full foliage or flower.

Major shrubs or trees should not be

removed without careful thought because maturity is a welcome ingredient of any garden and replacements may need some years of growth to fill the space. It should also be noted that any larger trees may be subject to tree preservation orders and the local authority must be consulted before any work is carried out.

Site and Local Conditions

It is readily appreciated that climate varies from extremes of north and south and that conditions vary enormously depending on the altitude and position of a garden. Less obvious is the fact that individual gardens show great variation in the protection which they offer compared with others in the immediate locality.

Low-lying areas are prone to frosts, and the upper slopes of hills are more subject to the destructive influence of the wind. Very little can be done to protect the whole garden from frost but it is possible to position susceptible plants where damage will be minimized. Wind also has a major cooling effect on plants as well as the purely mechanical damage which it can inflict, but proper placing of hedges, fencing and walls can provide effective shelter.

Soil

Newcomers to horticulture are inclined to believe that soil is really nothing more than soil, and many will also hold the view that it is a form of dirt. It may be dirty but it is also immensely variable and on it depends the success or failure of the plants which it supports. All soil, with the exception of peat areas, has a mineral origin and has been formed over millions of years by the action of ice, frost and rain on various kinds of rock. The particle size varies from the comparatively large grains of sand to the minute particles of clay which bind together into the unfriendly lumps that characterize some soils. Sand enables the rapid drainage of excess water while clay is effective in the long-term retention of moisture and so a mixture of these ingredients will form the basis of a suitable soil.

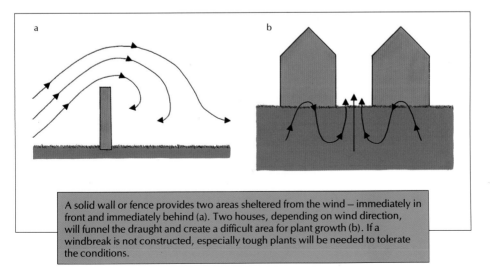

A solid wall or fence provides two areas sheltered from the wind — immediately in front and immediately behind (a). Two houses, depending on wind direction, will funnel the draught and create a difficult area for plant growth (b). If a windbreak is not constructed, especially tough plants will be needed to tolerate the conditions.

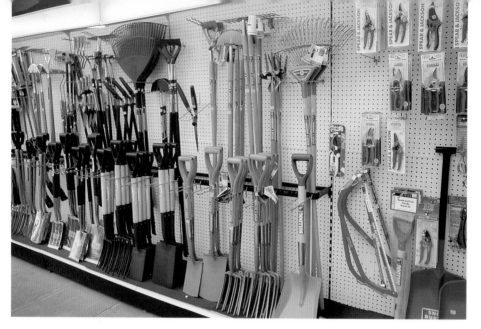

Most garden centres offer an enticing array of tools but they should be bought individually, as they are required.

However, the texture of soil is only one factor for growth as something else is needed to promote healthy and vigorous plants – fertility. This is dependent on the presence of what is known as humus, the end-product of decaying animal and vegetable matter. In the natural world, everything that lives will die and is gradually incorporated into the soil where the process of decay is brought about by countless millions of micro-organisms.

It follows that the way to improve garden soil and hence the success of plants is to incorporate organic material into the soil, and to this end every garden should aim to maintain a compost heap. Adding compost to the soil can be carried out as a little-and-often task or as an occasional 'blitz' but it should be appreciated that it is vital for garden improvement. There is the temptation, especially with small gardens, to buy a lorry load of fresh soil as a once and for all improvement but there are drawbacks. Good topsoil is available but it comes as a surprise to find how many loads are needed and at what cost *and* the beneficial effects will not last indefinitely.

Tooling up

The armoury of suitable weapons for engaging in gardening is not large although it is probably better to buy them as the need arises rather than to purchase a comprehensive selection at the beginning. A spade and a trowel are essential but many others may do nothing more than occupy space in the potting shed if they are bought from initial impetuosity rather than positive requirement.

It is important to handle tools before buying as this enables some judgement about size, weight and comfort to be made before decisions about price and quality. Stainless steel tools are generally the most desirable but spades and forks are very expensive and may not be sufficiently heavy for some users (this is particularly true of Dutch hoes). Good tools can last a lifetime and are a joy to possess and use but it is essential to use the right tool for the job, especially when heavy work is involved. Secateurs, for instance, will suffer if used on unduly thick stems; they will also deteriorate if they are not cleaned, oiled and sharpened on a regular basis.

2 • PLANNING

At an early stage, it becomes imperative to make some judgement about the scale of the projected operation with due regard to the part to be played by the gardener. For some, the task ahead may be too daunting and the employment of professional assistance may be required. Those who can confidently plan the garden, especially the hard landscaping – walls, paths and other construction work – can simply employ a local builder to carry out specific instructions. Alternatively, the planning, construction and planting can be left to an experienced landscape gardener. Here, some caution is needed because many of those who describe themselves as 'landscape gardeners' are often building practitioners who have little knowledge of plants. The true professional in this sphere has considerable

This garden has a large, formal pool but the dominant influence is that of paved areas and modern design.

The geometric designs of ornamental concrete blocks are varied but will convey a modern and formal design.

Virtually the whole of the garden can be 'hard landscaped' leaving a large patio area and reducing maintenance.

experience of garden plants and their effective deployment in domestic arrangements. Such people will work to a realistic price but it should be appreciated that a complete landscaping service will be expensive even for a small garden.

Hard Landscaping

Planning a garden and implementing the plan is great fun and well within the scope of normal mortals although it is understandable that some may have doubts. Most people would feel that, even as novices, they could achieve the objective of buying and putting the plants into their allotted positions but may feel apprehensive about laying pathways and building garden walls.

Although mainly paved, the wall plants and well-placed containers give an attractive and well-planted impression.

A feature wall can be surmounted by a metal or timber superstructure to support plants. This creates a high screen but allows a longer-distance view through the arch.

It would be wrong to say that no skill is required but common sense, care and patience are equally important; skill will make the job quicker, but a thoughtful and unhurried approach will allow anyone to succeed.

Perhaps the most vital decision is the choice of materials because in most cases there should be a sympathetic match with the house. This does not necessarily entail using the same kind of bricks for garden construction but the contrast should not be unseemly. Broadly, more modern buildings contrast strongly with traditional materials like natural stone, though there are many alternatives; similarly, older-style houses do not complement the pastel-coloured, artificial stonework which is currently available.

Where there is a slope to the garden, a feature wall makes a superb division, giving an illusion of increased size and affording the opportunity for making an abrupt change in garden style. A single-level terrace adds greatly to the interest of a garden arrangement but the amount of work involved in raising an area, even by only a few inches, is considerable. Low walls can be considered in flat gardens simply to add a further dimension to the scene or to enclose a raised flower-bed or part of a rockery.

The other decision to be made is whether the walls should be formal or otherwise and this will depend on the material and the relationship with the rest of the property. Modern concrete blocks demand a formal approach and the construction will almost always involve the use of a cement mortar, whereas natural stone and many of the artificial stone blocks lend themselves to more casual building techniques. Drystone wall construction becomes feasible and the use of soil infill secures the structure and provides the added interest of growing plants in the crevices.

The final thing to say about walls is that they offer considerable protection to plants; indeed, a walled garden was thought to be

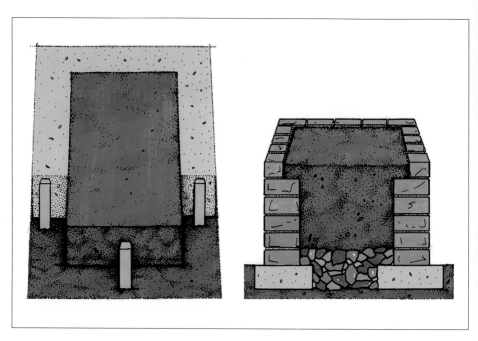

Raised beds are easily constructed.

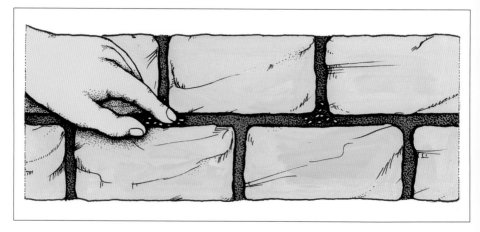

*Drystone walls are an especially useful feature for the small garden in that they
can be built to suit the size of the garden and are extremely practical: aside from
serving as dividers or wind-breaks, they can be used to grow plants. Sowing seed in
the crevices is a simple enough matter, but make sure that the seeds are placed at
the foot of a vertical joint, not at the top.*

essential in bygone times. It would be a major brick-laying project to enclose even a small garden and, perhaps more important, it would probably be an aesthetic failure. However, a short section of wall is useful close to the house or as an extending feature of a patio. In this case, its value would be appreciated as a sun-trap to protect tender plants and house owners!

Trellis and Pergola

Whereas garden walls have the real purpose of containing and supporting, the erection of a trellis or pergola is essentially cosmetic, giving extra opportunity to grow climbing plants. Suitably placed trellis-work is an effective screen for dilapidated sheds or compost heaps and although roses and clematis are often used to clothe the trellis, it should really have an evergreen component so that the screening is evident throughout the year.

Unless there is a positive reason for leaving the central area open, gardens large and small benefit from being partially obscured. When the overall view is partly limited by an attractive diversion, it adds an air of mystery and suggests hidden delights. It also means that everything in the garden is not revealed at a single glance and that a different viewpoint will offer a quite different view.

The use of trellis and climbing plants creates a pleasantly secluded enclosure.

Clematis need a trellis or other means of support . . . Comtesse de Bouchard is shown here.

A pergola is a much more substantial structure and while it can function as a 'plant corridor', it will also be regarded as a feature in its own right. It can be incorporated into the patio area to give increased privacy and will also give at least partial shade and the proximity of foliage and flowers. When used away from the house, a pergola becomes a visual highlight and, like a trellis, will serve as a taller screen to hide any eyesores, and allow a transition of garden style.

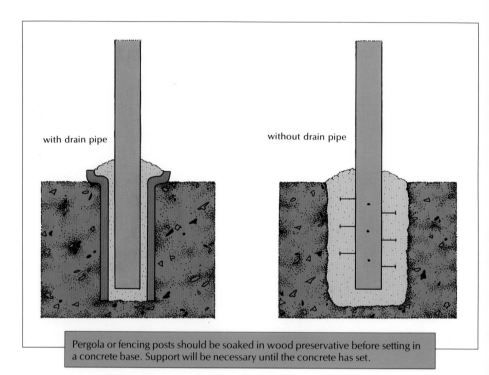

with drain pipe

without drain pipe

Pergola or fencing posts should be soaked in wood preservative before setting in a concrete base. Support will be necessary until the concrete has set.

A pergola needs to be constructed from strong rustic poles or sawn timber; it will offer considerable wind resistance when supporting plants in full leaf.

Steps and Paths

In some gardens, steps may be essential to provide convenient access to higher parts of the garden but even when slopes are minimal, steps can emphasize a change in level. A very small change in height can accommodate steps with risers of about 10cm (4in) and will make a pleasant focal point which can also be embellished by a small wall.

Paths are almost essential in all gardens if only to protect lawns and beds from the damage of foot traffic and to remove the necessity for special footwear for wet-weather visits to the garden. A straight path is geometrically efficient but does not have the aesthetic allure of one which curves and suggests an elongated perspective. If it winds out of sight, perhaps behind a projecting

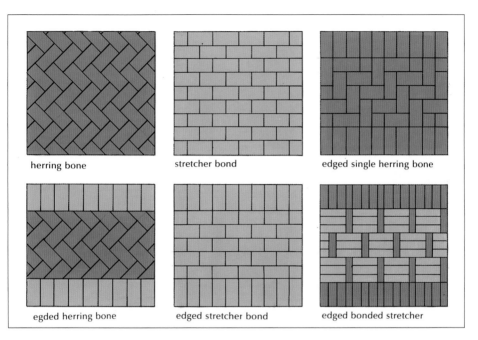

herring bone   stretcher bond   edged single herring bone

egded herring bone   edged stretcher bond   edged bonded stretcher

Pathways can be surfaced with bricks in various patterns.

flower-bed or shrubbery, it adds to the interest. Gardens are not only for displaying plants but also for harbouring illusions and creating impressions.

Again, there is considerable choice of materials, from the various styles of brick patterns to the delights of stone slabs or the undoubted practicality of ubiquitous concrete. Nowadays there are some proprietary drive and path surfaces which offer a variety of effects and although they are essentially pseudo, their appearance is attractive and long-lasting.

The DIY possibilities for pathmakers are endless and a visit to specialist supermarkets and garden centres will supply adequate inspiration for style and material. There is also no shortage of advice on construction methods. Ideally, this 'hard landscaping' should be completed before planting the garden but there is no real obstacle to a more piecemeal approach. Walls and paths may be considered as more permanent than plant arrangements but in reality they are not especially difficult to change later on.

Garden Boundaries

Boundaries have a special significance because they mark the extremities of the garden and symbolize the area of your domain. In most cases, walls, hedges or fences already exist and replacement or modification may not be necessary, but at some point consultation with neighbours becomes essential. The obligations of maintenance for party-fences will normally be set out in the house deeds but it is certainly advisable to reach an amenable agreement with neighbours so that the spirit as well as the letter of the law is observed.

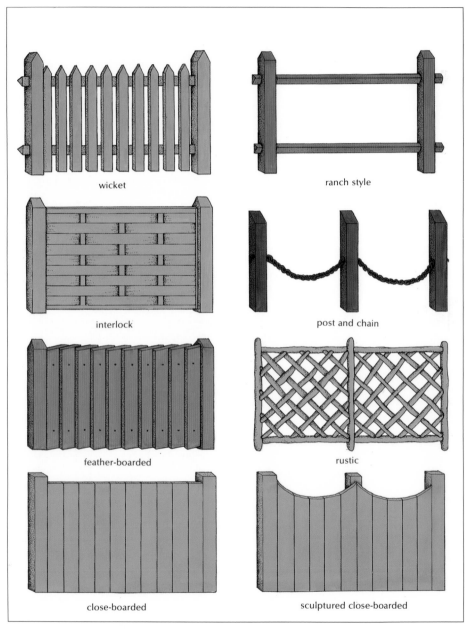

wicket

ranch style

interlock

post and chain

feather-boarded

rustic

close-boarded

sculptured close-boarded

Interlocking panels are perhaps the flavour of this age but there are many alternatives for wooden fencing.

The legal boundaries are one thing but it is equally important to give thoughtful consideration to those plants which are to grow close to the edges of the garden. You will not appreciate giant shrubs and trees planted in neighbouring gardens so that they rob your plants of root space and direct sunlight, therefore your own planning should adhere to the same principle.

In terms of design, those plants in adjacent gardens which are visible above fences and hedges do become an integral part of your own scene. If you are fortunate they will provide an attractive backcloth against which you can plan your own contribution.

The Shape of Things

The normal rectangular plot, especially in suburban areas, does dictate the visual design principles for gardens and does lead to a certain recognizable uniformity. In small front gardens the position of the garage and hence the driveway leave little scope for altering the conventional layout. Perhaps the only way of varying the impression is by allowing plants, at high and low levels, to overgrow the edges of the paths and drive and thus soften the outlines. If there is sufficient room for flower-beds and a small lawn, then both can be created

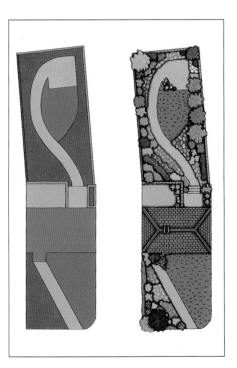

A long narrow plot needs a variety of shapes along the boundaries and pathways which distract the eye sideways rather than emphasizing the length of the garden.

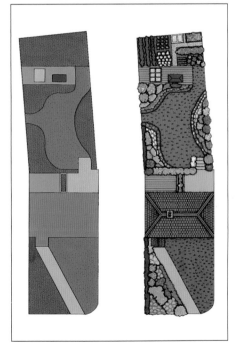

An alternative approach to the rear garden is to rely on the curves of flower-beds and an irregularly shaped lawn to disguise the rectangular influence. The length is deliberately foreshortened to accommodate cold frames and a vegetable area.

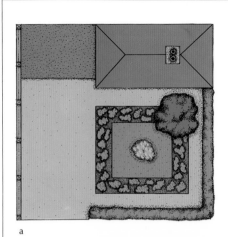
a

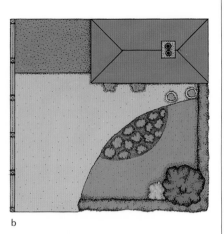
b

The front garden is almost invariably rectangular or square, and the design possibilities restricted still further by the position of the garage and driveway. Square beds (a) accentuate the rigid symmetry of the plot, while the curved bed and relocation of the tree in (b) have a softening effect and give the impression of greater space.

or converted to circular shapes as a minor rebellion against the linear layouts which tend to dominate.

The rear garden is more private and less influenced by neighbourhood tendencies and it is here that a greater freedom can be

The hard linear look of front gardens can be softened by allowing plants to overlap the drive edges and obscure part of the house.

expressed. Again the boundaries are almost sure to be linear but there are countless possibilities for conjuring a more natural delineation if this is desired. The easiest way to achieve a more casual effect is to vary the height and shape of those plants which are immediate to the boundary line.

An important consideration which is often and ironically overlooked is the principal viewpoint. If the garden will be most often viewed from the kitchen window or the patio, this should be a major reference point for the whole design. Don't forget, however, that even if one viewpoint dominates, there may be others which require thought. Can the sundial be seen to advantage? Is the fountain visible? Is the statue totally obscured? The layout for such highlights will be simplified by using a scale drawing and this will also help position all the main features planned. There are many themes which can form the centre-piece of a

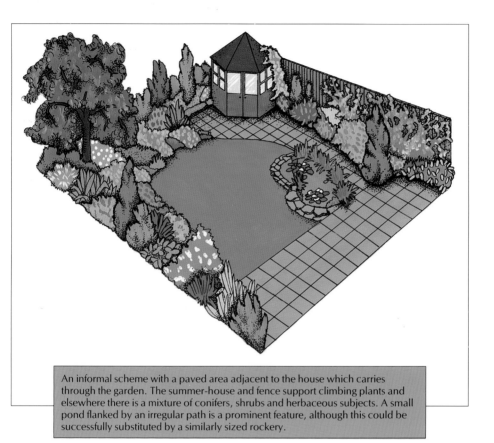

An informal scheme with a paved area adjacent to the house which carries through the garden. The summer-house and fence support climbing plants and elsewhere there is a mixture of conifers, shrubs and herbaceous subjects. A small pond flanked by an irregular path is a prominent feature, although this could be successfully substituted by a similarly sized rockery.

garden and some can be used jointly with great effect, but it is a mistake to expect a happy combination from numerous different features in a small area.

The best way to anticipate the effect of design features is to subject similarly sized gardens to critical scrutiny. In some cases they will provide real inspiration but there is much to learn from apparent failures: the rock garden looked too large, the pool was pitifully small and badly positioned, the rose bed was very bare, etc. Take the opportunity to see garden designs at the horticultural shows and, if it is convenient, look at the

examples in gardens such as Wisley, Kew and Harlow Carr, which are sure to give you ideas which can be used at home.

The next two chapters outline the various styles and features which make up the mainstream of current themes in domestic gardens. It is advisable to have some vision of what you hope to achieve though there is no need to be daunted by the apparent requirement to get it completely right at the outset. The best gardens, like the best ideas, are those which develop from sound principles and evolve with time and experience.

3 • FEATURES I

The Rose Garden

The ancient Greeks and the Romans were greatly enamoured of the rose; its appeal has lasted through the centuries and the flowers have become more beautiful. During the late nineteenth century, European rose species were interbred with those from China and Persia resulting in today's favourites, the hybrid teas. Alongside them are the floribundas, climbers, ramblers, miniatures and the less formal shrub roses, the latter now attracting more attention.

The high-centred, double blooms of the hybrid teas are the most admired flowers but it must be conceded that the bushes

A rose with a different habit of growth and luxuriant foliage . . . the shrub rose Ballerina.

Hybrid Tea roses are the most favoured flowers in the world, exemplified here by the beautiful variety Mullard Jubilee.

themselves are undistinguished and at some times of the year they are decidedly ugly. Consequently, a concentration of these plants needs careful siting and, ideally, the addition of underlying plants to provide some distraction from the gaunt stems of winter and early spring. Any of the early flowering and diminutive subjects such as pansies, primulas, polyanthus, bellis and a host of bulbous flowers will make a major display and short-statured bedding plants will perform a similar task in the summer.

Floribundas tend to exhibit the same bush deficiencies as hybrid teas but in both instances individual bushes can be grown successfully among shrubs and other plants. This enables mixed colours to be used more easily than is the case in beds devoted to roses alone where an assortment of varieties can clash quite badly. Hundreds of varieties are offered and it should be noted that there is considerable variation in the vigour and size of different cultivars. Many varieties of hybrid teas and floribundas can be purchased in the form of standards which have bare stems of 1.2 or 1.5m (4 or 5ft) in length. This extra height allows specimen roses to be grown at about eye-level and does not interfere with plants near the ground.

Miniature roses are frequently used in containers or rockeries but many other types of rose can succeed in large pots as long as the most vigorous varieties are not chosen. Shrub roses are very different both in habit and appearance, and even within the category there is variation between the rugosas, chinas, musks and damasks. Climbers have a particular purpose and are usually repeat-flowering but ramblers only flower in one flush and some varieties are especially prone to the mildew fungus. Neither of these two types is a true climber and will need training and tying to strong supports. In all cases, roses should be selected for specific sites to ensure that they do not outgrow their welcome.

Herbs

In recent years, herbs have undergone a revolution in popularity, not only for their culinary uses but also because they express a certain image. Some are small shrubs, others bulbs or small perennial plants and a number of them must be grown each year from seed but the common requirement is sunshine. All but the very largest can be grown well in containers and perhaps the

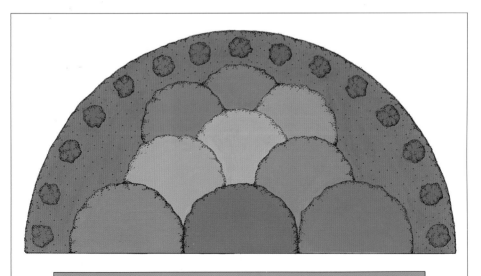

Suggested layout for a herb garden which is based on tiered planting with taller subjects at the rear. This design is semi-circular but any shape may be adopted to suit the garden.

Herbs are not only useful in the kitchen, the different leaf colours and textures are highly decorative and the plants grow well in pots.

mints should always be so confined because they are extremely invasive and will spread widely and quickly through the garden.

A small herb bed can easily be established using, for instance, the taller fennel, rosemary and sage as background perennials, fronted by marjoram and chives, with thyme used as edging. Space should be left for sowing the seed of basil, dill and parsley each year together with any others which are desired.

One rather contrived feature – which is both attractive and functional – is the herb cartwheel. The wheel is inserted into a circular bed with slates pushed vertically into the ground underneath the spokes, each segment being used for a different herb. Alternatively, inset bricks can serve the purpose of separating the plants.

The herb cartwheel is an excellent idea for the small garden, in that it is attractive and practical and yet does not take up too much space. It is also a useful way of introducing curves into the garden design.

Having outlined a couple of herb systems, it should be mentioned that all kinds can be grown in the open garden and will integrate handsomely among informal groups of decorative plants. Perhaps the only common exception is the somewhat expensive bay tree which is slightly tender and therefore benefits from being containerized and moved to a protected position near the house in winter.

The Small Tree and Shrub Garden

Whenever the topic of garden maintenance is raised, the profile of shrubs and trees is emphasized as being trouble-free, offering

Chaenomeles speciosa is the Japanese Quince and is one of the most versatile shrubs available. It thrives in all soils, in sun or shade and makes an excellent short hedge or wall plant; this species has bright red flowers in spring which are followed by yellow fruits in the autumn. There are several named varieties.

Trees must be chosen carefully for the small garden and many of the birches are very suitable. One slightly unusual one is Betula Golden Cloud which has soft yellow foliage and only reaches about twelve feet when mature.

the best results from the least work. There is an element of truth in the notion, evidenced by the widespread shrub borders on motorway fringes and the landscaping of public buildings in the name of low-cost maintenance. The danger, as frequently exemplified, is boredom and a lack of colour, and in a small garden devoted to shrubs and trees the danger is present. The gardener must call on as wide a variety of subjects as possible in order to offer a greater range of foliar effect and flowering capacity.

There is a huge range of choice in leaf colour, shape and textural effect, and a good plan will exploit the use of distinctive specimens which can be tall and slim, short and rounded, erect or cascading, and conifer or deciduous. The use of evergreens does avoid the totally denuding effect of winter but some moderation is needed because many evergreens can look rather sombre in the summer unless balanced with some bright colours. This is not so true of conifers which are found in a multitude of greens as well as greys, yellows or even blues.

A flower feast in spring is easily achieved with rhododendrons, magnolias, camellias and cherries but some subjects must be chosen for their summer display of flowers or foliage. Long-term flowers in the summer are more difficult to provide from shrubs and trees, and gardeners will rely on potentillas, hydrangeas and the shrubby mallows for this purpose. With all plants destined for a small garden, it is imperative to select on the basis of a long-lasting, quality performance; this is particularly necessary for shrubs and trees because they are among the most expensive of garden plants. Their planting and removal also entails more effort and consequently the initial choice should be given the appropriate consideration. Finally, as with roses and herbs, all trees and shrubs can be incorporated into a general garden scheme as well as being concentrated as a distinct feature.

The essence of a cottage garden is a profusion of plants low down but particularly at a higher level.

The Cottage Garden

Perhaps it is a statement about the time in which we live or maybe it is idealistic sentimentalism but there is an undoubted trend towards the cottage plan. Actually, it is characterized by an apparent absence of planning but this is far from true: although the emphasis is on informality, a great deal of care is needed in plant selection and arrangement. The traditional image of cottage gardens is usually that of a thatched roof and white walls but with some obvious limitations this type of garden can succeed for a modern house in suburban areas. However, the immediate setting is important and an estate with open-planned front gardens would present insuperable problems.

A cottage garden depends on profusion and an element of apparent confusion. The space should be filled, even crammed, at ground level and especially above because the essence is the taller rather than the shorter. Perennial subjects such as hollyhocks and foxgloves are interplanted with traditional annuals such as poppies and stocks. A few shrubs intermingled and a scattering of miscellaneous herbs with not a lawn in sight; it only remains to plant the rural pathway with thyme and provide discreet supports so that the house walls can drip with Virginia creeper and wisteria. There will, of course, be countless pots, sinks, hayracks and baskets . . . and perhaps a wooden wheelbarrow overflowing with bloom and foliage.

One note of warning: the cottage approach was never intended to provide an all-year-round display and if only the traditional plants are used, winter will look very bleak. Some carefully placed evergreens such as *Elaeagnus* and *Euonymus* will serve well for foliage and perhaps *Viburnum tinus* to offer some pretty flowers in the darkest months.

Two plants which will be in every cottage garden . . . the lupin in full sunshine and the foxglove in the shade.

Traditional hollyhocks (Althaea) were perennial plants but were often spoiled by rust disease and nowadays the varieties which are commonly grown are annuals or biennials. Some are stately spires reaching six feet in height but some are much shorter and do not require support. In all cases, the flowers are outstanding and appear from July until September.

The Formal Scheme

Strict formality in garden arrangements has been on the decline for some years, reflecting as it does a reliance on conformity and painstaking maintenance. Public parks have been the last resting-place but only a few, mostly in the tourist towns, have been able to resist the great pressures on expenditure. The clocks and heraldic designs which still exist are usually planted with carpet-bedding subjects which are grown to order and not often available to the gardening public. These plants are invariably foliage subjects which need constant trimming to maintain a sharp outline. This is also true of the small shrubs which comprise the old knot-garden schemes. Box is the first choice but both rosemary and lavender will tolerate the frequent use of shears to provide a dwarf-hedging effect.

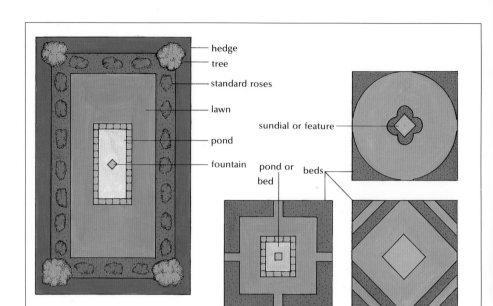

Formal schemes depend on symmetrical designs and if they are complicated, the maintenance is labour-intensive.

The schemes more likely to be found in parks and domestic gardens are better described as semi-formal because there is often a basically symmetrical layout. The beds have regular shapes, the varying heights of plants are tiered and there is often a consistent colour scheme. The numerous compact varieties of summer bedding plants are entirely adaptable for this use and so, too, are many of the most popular spring flowers.

Perhaps the appeal to home gardeners of a semi-formal design is that it conforms most readily with the common rectangular building plot with paths and drives running parallel to the boundaries. The result is rectangular lawns and rectangular flower-beds and, although this may be the result of an active decision, the suspicion remains that conscious design is absent and the joys of curves are unimagined.

The Sacred Sward

Few will argue with the idea that in Britain the lawn is a prerequisite to the essential garden layout. It undoubtedly makes a superb setting for garden plants and is a most versatile surface for children to play on and for adults to enjoy all manner of recreation. Unfortunately, in many gardens it is such a dominant element that it invites criticism of its decorative value. It is the most labour-intensive area of gardening and presents the greatest difficulties for those who aspire to a high-quality appearance. Mowing should occur at least twice a week from May until November; raking is necessary monthly during the same period; spiking is advisable every spring and autumn; light feeding should take place in the growing season and a top dressing is needed in the early winter. This amounts to a large

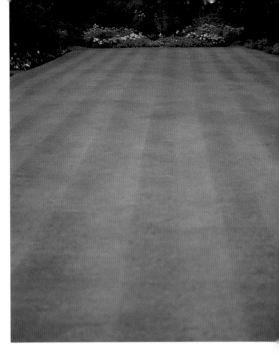

amount of work and no small expense for equipment and materials.

Over eighty per cent of British gardens have a lawn and, on average, grass covers about half of the total area. Most homes go to the expense of a power mower as well as other lawn tools, fertilizer and mosskiller. There is an illogicality which suggests that it is either a longstanding and unquestioned tradition or it is simply a love affair which defies analysis. Perhaps the best compromise plan is to mow as regularly as enthusiasm will allow (with a cylinder mower if the striped effect is wanted) and to devote what further time can be afforded on its cultivation. Do not expect to achieve a fine sward and remember that the greater the viewing distance, the better the grass will look. If you want to vary the theme, abandon straight lawn edges and cut some gentle curves.

Four out of five gardens have a lawn but high quality turf presents great difficulties for amateur gardeners.

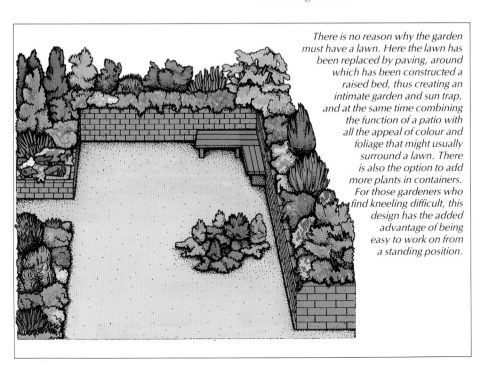

There is no reason why the garden must have a lawn. Here the lawn has been replaced by paving, around which has been constructed a raised bed, thus creating an intimate garden and sun trap, and at the same time combining the function of a patio with all the appeal of colour and foliage that might usually surround a lawn. There is also the option to add more plants in containers. For those gardeners who find kneeling difficult, this design has the added advantage of being easy to work on from a standing position.

4 • FEATURES II

The Patio

Twenty years ago the patio was a rarity in Britain when less than ten per cent of homes could claim one. Now the rate is above thirty per cent and it has become a definite requirement for many houses. Symbolically, it may represent the interface between home and garden but in practical terms it is a hard-surfaced area out of doors which is directly accessible from the house.

Ideally, the patio is above the level of the garden but this obviously depends on the lie of the land. Otherwise it is an extended path, usually at the rear of the house. A roughly south-facing aspect is desirable because direct sunshine is an essential ingredient for outdoor living. Often there is a screen on one or both sides as shelter against the wind and also to give more privacy. A partial overhead structure is sometimes included in the design to offer the shade which one hopes will be needed.

Plants are usually integrated into the plan, either planted where paving stones have been lifted or where concrete has been deliberately omitted. Containers can also be introduced. Screens and pergolas are obvious sites for climbing plants, and raised flower-beds or small walls can be constructed on the garden side of the patio. Hanging baskets and wall-mounted racks are attractive here, the only other necessities being the chairs and other casual furniture which can make patio life so pleasurable.

The Conservatory

Even using a kit, a conservatory is an

A stone-flagged patio which leads naturally into a rockery.

expensive addition to the home but it is a wonderful chance to experience a bright indoor lifestyle. Essentially it is an indoor patio where plants and people can share living space, although many conservatories have little vegetation. For many households, a conservatory is a home extension that offers external levels of brightness but internal standards of comfort and is frequently used as a sun lounge.

For the devoted gardener, a conservatory is a magical enclosure which allows the cultivation of warm-climate plants. These require a sustained level of warmth which would seem excessive for a greenhouse but quite reasonable for part of the dwelling. Even if the conservatory is not maintained at living-room temperatures, it will still be adequate for sustaining a huge range of sub-tropical vegetation through the winter months.

In terms of space, even the smallest garden can probably afford the 10 or 12sq m (110 or 130sq ft) which would be required for a modest conservatory. However, comparable expenditure would enable landscaping of a small garden together with the inclusion of the most expensive of plants. In short, the decision to invest in a conservatory will probably be more about financial resources than the limitations imposed by a small garden.

The Greenhouse

If a conservatory is for people but with plants in mind, a greenhouse can rightly be described as having the opposite emphasis. This does not imply that gardeners should not feel quite at home, for a glasshouse offers a superb combination of peace, solitude and protection from the elements. Nonetheless, gardening has practicality at its core and perhaps a greenhouse should be considered primarily as a major tool for the garden.

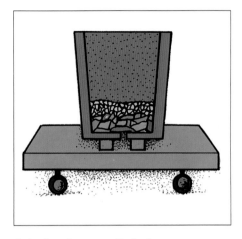

A simple trolley on small wheels or castors is helpful for the gardener who wants the freedom to rearrange heavy containers.

As such it is a tremendous boon to the activities which are imperilled by inclement weather: the cultivation of plants from seed and the propagation of other subjects from cuttings. It is especially important for the production of bedding plants because the seedlings and young plants need to be protected during the spring when the weather is at its most fickle. The cultivation of pot plants for the home is simplified and an abundance of fresh tomatoes can be supplied to the kitchen. The possibilities for vines, other choice fruit and a range of tender vegetables elevate the importance of a greenhouse for specialized crops and these also cover decorative plants such as late chrysanthemums, winter-flowering carnations and exhibition begonias.

The most popular size is 2.5m × 1.8m (8ft × 6ft) as anything smaller would be inconvenient, but larger is better in terms of value for money and perhaps 2.5m × 3m is the most sensible purchase. Such a greenhouse does not require elaborate foundations and neither must it be included in the

Pot plants raised from seed in a greenhouse; back row – zinnia, middle – gerbera, front – gazania.

further from the truth and even a tiny feature, if properly sited and constructed, can be pleasing to the eye and conducive to successful plants. The perfect situation would be a south-facing slope which is not shaded by tree or house and where the underlying soil is reasonably well drained. The size of the site will determine how large the component rocks should be; for a small area, it is unlikely that any will be difficult to handle. It is wise to mark out the project area with a length of hosepipe or string and then to decide on the highest level so that some estimate can be made for the amount of rock needed. If the rockery is going to be

shopping list when the garden is first established: buy a greenhouse when your enthusiasm justifies it.

The Rock Garden

Visitors to some botanical gardens may come away with the belief that a rockery is an immense undertaking which cannot be duplicated on a smaller scale. Nothing is

A planted stone sink fits very well into the low rockery which is nicely balanced by the dark foliage of the hedge.

Individually designed rockeries can easily incorporate a pathway to give aesthetically pleasing access.

positioned next to the patio, it is desirable to ensure that it is constructed in a similar style and, if possible, that it is built from the same materials.

For a low rockery, it may be necessary to excavate the underlying soil and incorporate some 20 or 23cm (8 or 9in) of rubble to ensure good drainage. With higher structures, excess water will not be held, especially if care is taken to include large quantities of grit and sharp sand with the infill soil. A covering of chippings will add to the appearance and will also ensure the drier surface which alpine plants prefer. True alpine plants are not the only subjects which grow successfully in rockeries and many more common plants are perfectly suitable. Indeed, some of the smaller bedding or perennial plants are essential for providing summer flowers because most alpines are at their best in the spring.

Random stone walling gives the opportunity to grow a selection of plants in crevices.

This rockery is at its best in spring with the wonderful backcloth of tree blossom and fresh green foliage.

Water Gardening

Water does introduce something special to gardens by adding a totally different texture which mirrors the changing light and reflects the contrast of sky colours. Moving water is as attractive to the eye as the sound is soothing to the ear. None of these pleasures is exclusive to streams and lakes but can be represented by small pools, tiny cascades, miniature fountains and simple water spouts. A pond is a considerable attraction to wildlife and even if fish are not introduced, frogs, toads, newts and aquatic insects will surely appear. Water-lilies can be planted in the pond with marginal plants around the edges and thus a whole new world of vegetation can be displayed in the garden.

There are numerous pre-designed pools available which are constructed from fibre-glass but sheet butyl liners will give total flexibility of design. The basic choice is between formal and informal shapes to match the overall plan of the garden or the specific area where the pool is planned.

Often listed as a marginal or pool-side plant, the astilbe does enjoy moist soil but is quite happy anywhere in the garden. The beautiful spires of bloom can be red, pink, cream or white and the foliage is equally appealing. Perhaps the best place for astilbe is in difficult shady corners where it does remarkably well.

This versatile feature offers a raised pool
with fish, fountain, water-lilies and an
integral seat, and yet is capable of fitting
into the smallest garden.

An economy-sized corner pool with
ornamental spout which can be decorated
to become the focal point of patio or
garden.

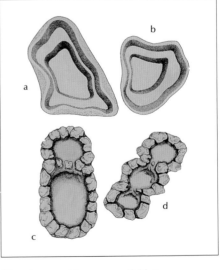

Fibreglass mouldings are available in
many different shapes and sizes. Some are
plain but with a built-in shelf and an
overlap rim which can be covered with
soil or stones (a and b). Others are more
complex designs with multiple pools and
imitation rock surrounds.

Running water requires the complication of a pump which can be sited in an underground cavity or under the water but must also be supplied by a power cable from the mains electricity in the house. Careful planning is essential for any water feature and there will always be a fair amount of manual labour involved in either digging out soil or constructing a raised pool. So many options exist for including water in the garden that it would be prudent to visit a specialist garden or aquatic centre to select equipment and to obtain advice.

Fruit and Vegetables

Conventional aesthetics dictate that vegetables are unseemly when grown in the decorative garden, and generations of gardeners have set aside a separate plot for the purpose. Invariably, this area is screened from view as if vegetables are a cultivated embarrassment which should be tasted but not seen. Perhaps modern cultivators have abandoned this mentality but, if not, remember that sunshine is important to success and a secluded and shady area will not serve well. The majority of edible crops are easily cultivated, although carrots need a light soil and cauliflowers require extra care and a really good soil. Almost all the others can be attempted with confidence, and where ground space is limited nobody should hesitate to use containers.

Fruit is similarly tainted with the reputation of poor visual attraction, although many apples and pears are given limelight

Fruit trees are extremely decorative in the spring, ably supported by tulips and wallflowers in the beds.

positions to display their spring blossom. Soft fruit such as currants and gooseberries are normally relegated to hidden positions but they are not without some visual charm. Raspberries are indeed a nuisance, not for their looks but because they will not be confined to their allotted space and will quite quickly spread to all parts of the garden if not forcibly restrained.

Other cane fruits such as loganberries, tayberries and blackberries can come into their own on fences and walls because the annual growth can be trained in any

convenient direction. Covering drab surfaces with pleasant and fast-growing foliage, they also produce a really abundant crop. One other plant worth special mention is the blueberry; if the soil is acid (and it must be) this uncommon fruit hosts beautiful flowers in the spring and gives an outstanding display of foliar brilliance in the autumn. The fruit is a delicious bonus – if the birds leave any!

Strawberries must also be included in this brief outline because of the popular position they occupy with the eating public. They are simply grown, even in slight shade, in the garden but the greatest success is achieved in the special pots which are designed to accommodate more than a dozen plants. In the garden, the strong perfume attracts destruction by birds and slugs but the elevated protection of strawberry 'towers' deters these creatures.

Most famous of the *Prunus* family are the flowering cherries which come in a large variety of shapes and sizes. Most are conventional trees which can grow over twenty feet in height with an even greater spread though some are quite slender columns which look superb when covered in spring blossom. Many flowering cherries have distinctive bark and often colourful foliage in autumn.

Containers that have been specially designed for growing strawberries can be used earlier in the year for displaying small bulbs or spring plants.

There is a huge range of containers constructed from a variety of materials which provides a choice to suit every garden design and individual situation.

Containers

Without any soil at all, it is possible to have the most enchanting, decorative garden or the most productive edible results by using plant containers. Pots, tubs, window-boxes, wall and hanging baskets and a host of improvised receptacles can put much of the world's vegetation at your disposal. Clearly there are tropical plants that will not thrive in low temperatures but back yards, balconies and some terraces are in the proximity of heated buildings and close to the protection of substantial walls. It is surprising what subjects succeed in containers and a lack of variety is not a problem with this type of gardening. The other major benefit is that plants become 'mobile' and can be moved to different positions at different times of the

This very small front garden is exploited to the full by using pots and boxes wherever possible.

Balconies and other hard surface areas are easily made colourful with petunias, geraniums and Busy Lizzies.

year to take advantage of extra shelter or extra exposure.

The biggest difficulty is maintaining a proper water supply, especially during sunny, dry and fairly breezy weather; even when there is rain, it is not usually sufficient

Householders with or without gardens can indulge a passion for flowers by using a window-box.

The roof garden offers an excellent opportunity for making the most of container gardening. Here there is the added benefit that the surrounding walls offer ideal support for climbing plants.

Evergreens will decorate containers throughout the year and require little maintenance, especially during winter.

to satisfy strongly growing plants. The physical effort of filling the watering can and dispensing its contents can become arduous and anyone with a large number of containers should make arrangements for a hosepipe. With an external water supply and a flexible hose, it is fairly simple to organize a drip feed – through small holes – to numerous containers.

Many container gardeners are content to concentrate on spring and summer ornamentals for their pleasure but there is no obstacle to planting evergreens and other winter interest subjects. Not only are they decorative throughout the year, but they need no maintenance in periods of slow growth and they can be supplemented with temporary flowering plants at various times.

Large containers like tubs and window-boxes can be filled with plants which remain in their individual pots so that replacement when necessary is easy. Placed on a layer of pebbles and surrounded with peat or compost, the pots will be well drained and protected from undue loss of moisture.

Miscellaneous Gardens

It seems likely that most gardens will fall into this category in the sense that they were not truly planned but rather laid out when the house was built and have not subsequently evolved to any great extent. Most will contain more than one of the common features without any being really dominant. Poor-quality grass will cover about half the area, roses and other shrubs will be present with perhaps a tree and there will be a container in use. Patios are becoming commonplace, greenhouses are in almost one in twelve gardens and conservatories may soon be as numerous. A vegetable patch exists in less than half our gardens, fruit grows in about a third of them, rockeries are far less common and water features are still quite rare.

With patio, pergola, lawn, steps, walls, beds, shrub borders and a lean-to greenhouse, this small garden has been well planned.

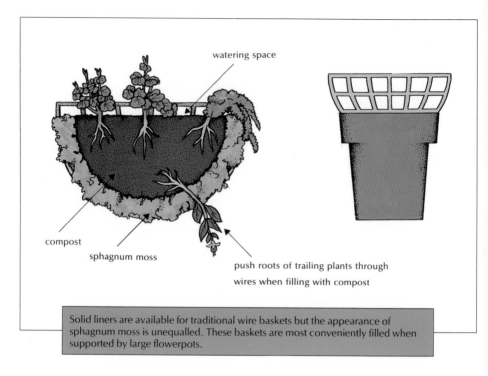

watering space

compost

sphagnum moss

push roots of trailing plants through
wires when filling with compost

Solid liners are available for traditional wire baskets but the appearance of
sphagnum moss is unequalled. These baskets are most conveniently filled when
supported by large flowerpots.

*A priority for many gardeners is to provide
a floral welcome at the front door.*

There is an increasing awareness of the
difficulties faced by wildlife and a greater
appreciation of general environmental issues.
Gardeners are less inclined to use toxic
sprays and are more familiar with wild flowers; many more of these are now cultivated
but there has not been any widespread adop-
tion of 'wilderness gardening'. Some gardens
make the gesture of having an untended
corner where nature will prevail but this is
more symbolic than effective. A good deal
of wildlife is nurtured by suburban gardens
and gardeners should not feel guilty about
the fact that they cultivate a preponderance
of overseas, rather than indigenous plants.
Our planet will not decline because of
anything taking place in gardens and we
should hope that the concerns of gardeners
are reflected in the world at large and that
their attitudes will influence the important
decisions which must be taken.

5 • PLANT SELECTION AND SITING

The range of plants which is available to the home gardener is quite staggering, and for the beginner making decisions can be perplexing. Reading catalogues and gardening books does ease the confusion, but only by seeing the plants can sensible choices be made. The most important factor is aesthetic appeal but try to avoid buying plants on impulse as this can lead to disappointment or to an expensive error. Having earmarked a certain plant, it is vital to ensure that the proper conditions can be provided to cater for that particular species.

All plants have evolved over hundreds of thousands of years and their specific needs depend on the climatic conditions which have fashioned them. All have temperature limitations and will only succeed within a certain range but plants are also critically disposed towards residual moisture around the roots and to the intensity and cumulative duration of sunlight. For instance, it is well recognized that cacti grow in semi-desert areas where there may be little annual rainfall. These specialized plants are able to store water and have extensive root systems to absorb what little moisture that

By choosing the right position for plants, they are given the chance to do their best, like these lavatera and begonias.

There are not a great number of shrubs which flower for a long period over the summer and the hydrangea is exceptional. Pinks, reds, blues and whites are available but colour is complicated by the soil acidity. Acid soil turns the flowers blue and alkaline conditions make them pink or red. Colourants are sold to add to the soil.

exists. Cacti survive where other plants could not but it should be realized that if the climate changed from arid to permanently wet, the cacti would die out and be replaced by vegetation which was suited to the new conditions.

To a lesser degree, all other plants have particular requirements and where they are met, successful growth will take place. Many subjects have considerable tolerance to a variety of climatic conditions as well as soil differences but some are very particular indeed. Having decided on the plant which pleases, it is imperative that its cultivation profile is checked. Does it prefer a shady or sunny position? Should the soil be fairly dry and well drained or is permanent moisture required? Is lime needed in the soil or should it be quite acidic?

Shade

Even if a garden is stocked with low-growing plants, there will still be areas which are shaded by the house, shed, fences or hedges. It is also likely that trees and shrubs in neighbouring gardens will obscure some direct sunlight for at least part of the day. Depending on the type of foliage canopy, the shade can be dense, partial or dappled and gardeners should familiarize themselves with the differing areas. With a 'shade map' of the garden, it will be much easier to decide on the types of plant that are likely to do well in the various situations.

Some suburban gardens and many town gardens may be completely obscured from direct sunshine, perhaps in summer as well as in winter. While this is certainly a limiting factor, there is a wide range of plants that relish permanent shade, although it will be difficult to ensure a profusion of summer flowers.

Bear in mind that any tall feature or shrub that you add to the garden will have an effect on the amount of light and shade available to other plants in the garden. This is an important consideration that is frequently overlooked at the design stage.

The constraints of small front gardens can be eased by the slight informalities of taller plants and a rounded lawn.

Sunny Areas

If sitting out in the garden is a priority, the first consideration must be to reserve the requisite space in a suitable position. Other allocations of sunny places can be made for appropriate plants but remember to make some allowance for the climatic context of the garden. Some shade-loving plants may tolerate the sunniest gardens in Glasgow but they would be severely stressed by the intensity and relatively persistent sunshine in the Isle of Wight. Every gardener needs to make some judgements based on local observations until such time as the knowledge of experience can guide future planting but sometimes the only way to find out is to try.

Wet and Dry

Clearly, there are some plants which need abundant supplies of water; the aquatic species which must be grown in water are the extreme example. In the garden, wetness will depend not only on rainfall but also on how effectively water drains away and passes through the soil. If the land slopes, drainage should be good but if the garden is at the bottom of a slope, wet conditions will prevail unless the soil is extremely porous or a drainage system is installed.

Sandy soils retain little moisture and this deficiency should be improved by incorporating regular amounts of organic material. However, in some areas of Britain, the rainfall ensures that even sandy soils will rarely dry out. The Thames estuary may attract 50cm (20in) of annual rainfall, whereas the figure for parts of Scotland, Wales and the Lake District can be above 375cm (150in).

In the same way that sandiness will often result in dryness, heavy clay soils are rightly often associated with wetness. Exceptional

Hostas are highly versatile plants which prefer shady and moist positions but will do almost as well in open sunny spots if the soil does not dry out frequently. The flowers are pale but quite attractive, although the hosta is famed for its veined leaves which are often variegated. Quite a few different varieties exist and all are simply propagated by dividing the clumps.

conditions do occur and dried-out clay is probably the most unaccommodating of soils but, ironically, the long-term cure for clay is the same as that used to improve sand: large quantities of organic waste.

Where a garden is seriously wet – to the extent that it is often waterlogged – drainage systems can be built and, obviously, serious dryness can be countered by a watering system. Even if the situation seems extreme, there is no doubt that counter-measures are possible and that plants will be able to thrive. The worst possible combination of factors is to be found in areas of less than moderate rainfall, when plants are extremely difficult to establish under the shade of major trees.

Hot and Cold

Temperature, like the other elements of climate, depends on latitude, altitude, the proximity of the sea and the prevailing wind direction and there is very little that

the gardener can do about these things. However, in the British Isles the variation is wide, from the almost sub-tropical parts of the south-west where the nearby Gulf Stream almost precludes frost to the almost sub-arctic region of north-east Scotland. The palm trees of Cornwall would be unsuited to the Aberdeen coastline but the range of intervening possibilities gives an immense range of plant choice. Added to that is the microclimate of the garden which can be used to good effect for protecting susceptible plants from damaging cold.

The house itself behaves like a huge radiator and will allow quite tender subjects to succeed when grown against the walls or even a few feet away. Trees, sheds, hedges and fences will act as windbreaks and shield foliage from the chill factor of adverse winds. Usually, these are from a northerly or easterly direction and their influence over plant growth is enormous. Special precautions against winter winds involve the use of peat coverings or wrappings with straw or insulating plastics, although many gardeners believe these measures to be too intrusive.

In Britain, outdoor plants do not suffer much with heat stress, although it can be common under glass. However, there are exceptional periods when intense sunshine coincides with a prolonged drought. Root dryness allied with high temperatures can kill or damage even well-established plants and the danger will be indicated when the plant begins to flag. In this process, the foliage, flowers and young stems begin to wilt but this is a perfectly natural way of reducing water loss and the plant will resume its turgidity after it is watered.

Acidity and Alkalinity

Gardeners are in the business of growing attractive and healthy plants and good fertile soil is a prerequisite to this end. Results

A special but inexpensive clip converts two panes of glass or sheets of transparent plastic into a cloche, giving shelter from excess rain or light frost. It is erected and dismantled quickly.

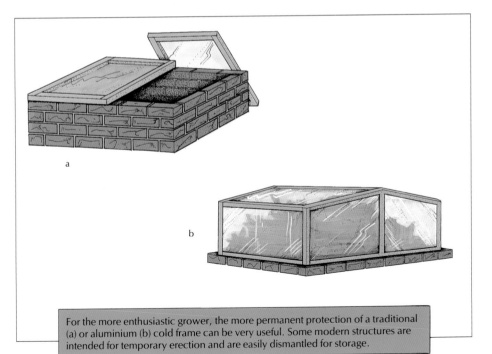

For the more enthusiastic grower, the more permanent protection of a traditional (a) or aluminium (b) cold frame can be very useful. Some modern structures are intended for temporary erection and are easily dismantled for storage.

One plant which needs an acid soil is the azalea.

A pH test kit will enable you to establish the acid/alkaline content of the soil, a factor which will to a large extent determine your choice of plants.

can be seriously affected, however, by the presence or otherwise of lime. Acidity and alkalinity is measured on the pH scale which ranges from 1 to 14 with number 7 indicating neutral and number 1 being the most acidic. The majority of soils are within 4 to 7.5 and the vast majority of plant species can be cultivated successfully over that part of the scale, but those plants which favour the extremes will sicken in other situations.

Some people do shy away from the scientific aspects of gardening and it must be said that the generations of former times were highly effective in managing their crops without scientific data. Nowadays, soil analysis kits are commonplace and they are simple to use and give adequately precise readings, removing the element of guesswork and the requirement for lengthy cultivation experience.

Most garden soils are at least slightly acidic and the process of adding organic compost will maintain the same level or only slightly increase it unless lime is added. Generally, the nearer to neutral, the greater the range of plants which thrive and this means that lime must be added very occasionally for the best results. Vegetable growers will probably use lime every year because acid soil prevents many nutrient chemicals being available to most common edible crops. Potatoes and chicory are notable exceptions but, even in these cases, some lime should be added occasionally because of its beneficial effect on soil fertility. On the other hand, those gardens which treasure rhododendrons, camellias and heathers would not jeopardize such plants by adding lime at any time to their growing areas.

Soil chemistry is undoubtedly a complicated business and the detail need not concern gardeners, but it would be foolhardy to be unaware of the requirements of plants in this respect or not to know the pH of the soil in which they will be planted. If existing plants are not growing well, there could be many reasons and the prudent cultivator would want to ascertain whether excess acidity or alkalinity was responsible. The pH of soil is easily raised by adding lime and it can also be lowered, though with rather more difficulty, by the use of peat, composted waste and some chemicals.

Selecting the plants which will have the best opportunity for success is so important that perhaps a brief résumé would be helpful. They should satisfy the requirements for being attractive, fulfil the considerations of size and shape and have a suitable profile for the soil and climatic conditions. Ideally, every plant would be supplied with a comprehensive label which specified the essentials: wet or dry, sun or shade, height and spread, hardiness or tenderness and also the pH preference. In the absence of such labels, it is incumbent on the purchaser to seek the appropriate advice from the nursery or garden centre or from books and catalogues.

Where conditions are not ideal for a particular plant, its quality of growth will deteriorate over a period of time. Sometimes, but not always, it will lead to the death of a plant but this will only occur rapidly if the planting position is grossly unfavourable, perhaps because of total dryness or waterlogging. A soil which is too acid or too alkaline will rarely result in a

Choisya ternata, the Mexican Orange Blossom, is a serious contender for the title of best shrub. The tidy, rounded bush has pretty, evergreen leaves which are fragrant, and scented flowers which mostly appear in spring but thereafter in the summer. It grows to about six feet tall and with equal spread but does not resent pruning and although it prefers an open, sunny site, it performs well in partial shade. There is some doubt about its hardiness in cold climates and it will benefit from the protection of a wall. The species is illustrated but there is a new golden variety called Sundance.

quick death and, instead, there will be a gradual reduction of vitality, resulting in unhealthy foliage and stunted growth. This long-term decline is especially apparent with regard to major plants like trees, shrubs and large perennials, while those which are more temporary, such as the annuals, will often survive their normal term but without achieving their full potential.

6 • PLANTING AND PROPAGATING

Planting

Buying the best plants is an obvious starting-point but careless and untimely planting can be a costly and wasteful effort because it fails in the objective of giving the plant its best possible beginning to garden life. Soft material like bedding plants has no stringent requirements but more expensive and expansive subjects, such as shrubs and trees, deserve proper attention.

Many plants may be purchased as containerized, pot-grown or with balled roots and as such they represent the most versatile types for planting purposes. In general, they can be planted at any time of the year but that advice should not supersede common sense. Planting in very wet weather will damage the structure of the soil which will seriously compact around the roots. In frosty weather, it will be impossible to ensure that the roots are brought into full contact with the surrounding soil.

The principal aims are to plant at the same depth as the plant has been grown and, having dug a comfortably sized hole, to accomplish firm contact between root and soil. Where container and pot-grown plants are concerned, it is an excellent practice to include a generous amount of peat in the hole as many subjects will have been grown in peat-based composts. In all cases, the addition of peat, bark or garden compost is helpful to root expansion and will also raise the soil fertility around the new plant.

Some plants are still sold bare-rooted and should only be planted in the dormant season, normally between autumn and spring and when the weather permits. The roots should be examined and any damage cut away. If there are signs that any are shrivelled or that the top growth is dry, the plants must be submerged in water for at least a couple of hours. If the weather is unsuitable for planting, the plants can either be stored in a frost-free garage or shed, or

If immediate planting is not possible, bare-rooted plants should be 'heeled in', placing them in a shallow trench with the roots covered by a few inches of soil. This covering will protect them from dryness or frost until planting takes place.

'heeled in', a process which entails covering the roots with a few centimetres of soil in a shallow trench.

When planting taller subjects a suitable stake is needed and common sense urges that the stake is inserted before the plant so that root damage is avoided. Stem and stake are then secured, preferably with one of the proprietary ties which facilitate adjustment in the future.

A useful tip for planting climbers or wall shrubs against the house is to place the rootball about 30cm (1ft) away from the wall. The wall and the overhanging gutter often create a rain-shadow and the soil underneath may be very dry.

Large plants should have the hole infilled with a reasonably dry soil and peat mixture which can then be firmed by treading it down. This procedure can be followed with larger herbaceous plants but bedding and other small subjects should be firmed with hand pressure only when covering the roots.

In all cases, the final act of planting is generous use of the watering can which not only supplies the life-giving liquid but also washes particles of soil into any spaces

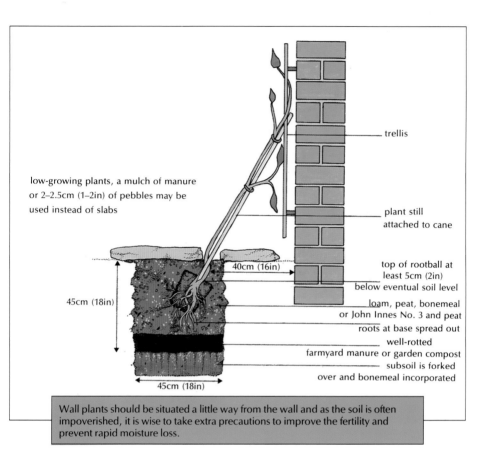

trellis

low-growing plants, a mulch of manure
or 2–2.5cm (1–2in) of pebbles may be
used instead of slabs

plant still
attached to cane

40cm (16in)

top of rootball at
least 5cm (2in)
below eventual soil level

45cm (18in)

loam, peat, bonemeal
or John Innes No. 3 and peat

roots at base spread out

well-rotted
farmyard manure or garden compost

subsoil is forked
over and bonemeal incorporated

45cm (18in)

Wall plants should be situated a little way from the wall and as the soil is often impoverished, it is wise to take extra precautions to improve the fertility and prevent rapid moisture loss.

around the roots. The wet soil will stick to the root hairs and allows the most efficient transfer of water into the plant. Rain may take over in the following days but when this does not occur, artificial irrigation is essential. The proper establishment of all new plantings depends on adequate watering; for shrubs and trees, the risk period can extend to some months and even the following year, if rainfall has been light.

Propagation

For many experienced gardeners, propaga-

tion is the most intriguing element in horti-culture and gives a happy impression of getting something for nothing. It has suffi-cient mystery to lend some uncertainty to its techniques but success is attainable by all and brings considerable pleasure. The own-ers of a small garden may feel that once planted, their beautiful patch will not require further attention, but this is not so. Gardens respond to the right treatment at the right time and this means that old plants will be removed, promiscuous ones pruned and failures will be replaced; herbaceous plants, especially, must be periodically rejuvenated and revitalized.

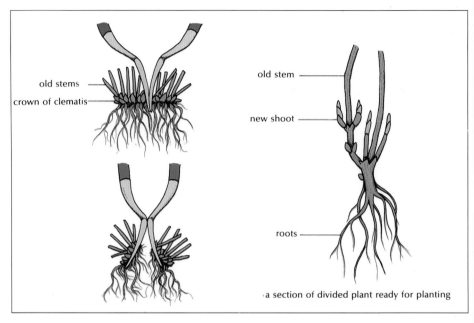

old stems

crown of clematis

old stem

new shoot

roots

a section of divided plant ready for planting

Tough clumps of perennials can more easily be divided by using two garden forks to lever the plant apart.

Division

The typical growth pattern of garden perennials is an ever-increasing clump which will inevitably begin to trespass on the space occupied by other plants. The expanding growth indicates good health, but after some years it will be found that the centre, which is the oldest part of the plant, will have lost vitality and may have started dying off. When this is detected, it is advisable to dig the clump out in the autumn or early spring and replant one or more pieces taken from the perimeter where the youngest parts of the plant are.

Splitting the plant, either by teasing pieces apart by hand or merely pushing a spade through an outer section, is an important method of rejuvenation and enables the old and perhaps unhealthy portions to be discarded. If the plant has been successful and admired, it may be desirable to introduce it to other parts of the garden and the newer portions can be divided into smaller pieces. Known as division, this form of propagation can be applied to all those plants which form clumps, and sections of plants can be removed without the necessity of digging up the whole of the parent plant.

Taking Cuttings

Division reproduces the parent plant exactly and so, too, does taking cuttings. There are different kinds of cuttings but the principle is straightforward: to take a leaf, bud, stem or section of root and grow a new plant from it. In each case, it is a clone from the parent plant and will be identical to it when mature. Some plant species will propagate more readily from one kind of cutting

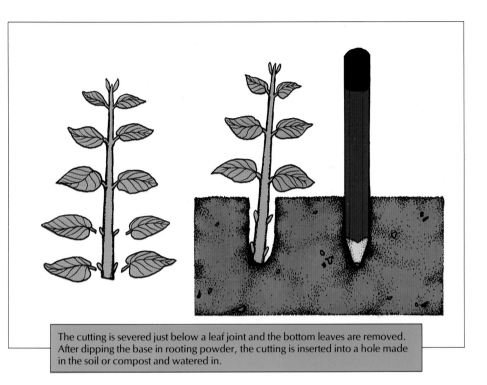

The cutting is severed just below a leaf joint and the bottom leaves are removed. After dipping the base in rooting powder, the cutting is inserted into a hole made in the soil or compost and watered in.

than from another but many will reproduce happily from more than one type of cutting.

The season determines the nature of stem cuttings; the softwood cuttings are taken early in growth when tip and stem are green and soft, whereas the hardwood kind are taken at the end of the year when the stem has become woody and hard. There is also an in-between condition known as half- or semi-ripe where the tip of the stem is soft while the lower portion is beginning to harden.

Herbaceous plants are usually propagated from softwood cuttings in the spring and they need to be planted in a pot of sandy soil and then watered. Ideally, they would be placed in a propagating frame which will provide warmth and a moist atmosphere to prevent the cutting from becoming dessicated. Otherwise, the pot of cuttings can be placed in a plastic bag and kept in a shady and protected spot near the house. The theory is that the moisture-laden atmosphere will sustain the cutting until new roots have formed in the compost.

Shrubs and trees tend to root more reliably from semi-ripe or hardwood cuttings taken in the late summer or the autumn. In this case, the sustenance for the new plant is in the structure of the mature stem, and the roots will form over a period of some months. Ripe cuttings of hardy plants are inserted a few centimetres deep in a shallow trench of prepared soil in a sheltered part of the garden.

All kinds of stem cuttings are made by cutting shoots just below a leaf node — where the leaves join the stem. The strongest hormonal activity takes place at this point and encourages the growth of roots from those cells close to the cut tissue. It is also advisable to remove all but three or four leaves from a cutting so that less water is lost through transpiration. The secret of success, if it is one, is to take the different kinds of cuttings at various times of the year as a way of hedging the bet! Some subjects are notoriously awkward to root but different approaches and persistence will usually bring success. Those which refuse to root by means of conventional cuttings can often be propagated by layering.

Layering

Cuttings cannot be said to be a natural process of plant procreation but layering frequently occurs in the wild. Basically, a flexible branch or stem is brought into contact with the soil and held there by a peg or a stone. The process is enhanced if the stem is partly cut and actually positioned in the soil at this point. This 'damage' will promote root growth, and the portion of intact stem will nourish and sustain the shoot indefinitely. Keeping the area of contact permanently moist will hasten rooting; this is greatly helped by using a flat stone and also by watering in dry weather. When the stem has visible roots and is clearly self-sufficient, it can be severed from the parent plant and replanted. Layering can take quite a few months but the success rate is very high even with difficult plants.

With layering and cuttings, it is often advisable to use hormone rooting powders to assist nature. Although they are not essential, the chemicals can induce roots to form more quickly and the accompanying

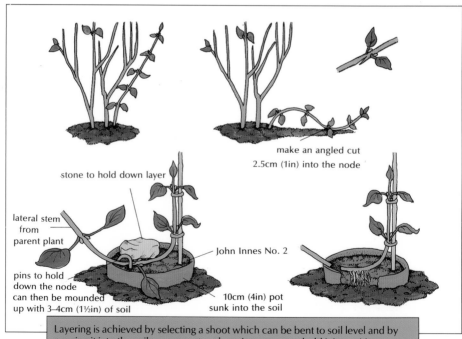

make an angled cut
2.5cm (1in) into the node

stone to hold down layer

lateral stem
from
parent plant

John Innes No. 2

pins to hold
down the node
can then be mounded
up with 3–4cm (1½in) of soil

10cm (4in) pot
sunk into the soil

Layering is achieved by selecting a shoot which can be bent to soil level and by pegging it into the soil or compost, or by using a stone to hold it in position.

fungicide will inhibit disease invasion of the exposed plant tissue.

Seed

Although some plants produce runners which root some distance from the parent plant and others expand their growth in outward regeneration, the most successful means of propagation is sexual. This involves participation between separate individual plants and allows the hereditary changes which result in evolution which could not take place with vegetative reproduction. Plants, like animals, have practised sexual reproduction for millions of years but whereas many animals have evolved to live-bearing status, seed is the preferred system for vegetation. Only a few species of plants can produce miniature young.

There is something quite fascinating about a tiny capsule which has the capability of becoming a mature plant and its development is one of the great joys of horticulture. Nonetheless, the use of seed by amateur growers is declining and this is a pity because it enables a huge range of plants to be grown which are not otherwise available. Perhaps this is a sign of the times which favours 'instant' plants, or it may also be that many gardeners have experienced disappointment with their seed-raising endeavours.

Seed may not always be of the best quality and, in some cases, it is too old for a high percentage of viability. If poor results are obtained when the instructions have been followed, a vigorous complaint should be made to the seed company who will always replace or refund. Sometimes the cultivator is to blame, perhaps for being more ambitious than his/her equipment or experience will permit. Some quite common seed does require a temperature of between 21 and 24°C (70 and 75°F) to be maintained steadily for two or three weeks.

An electrically heated propagator, preferably controlled by thermostat, is a desirable tool for germinating seed and rooting cuttings.

Only a thermostatically controlled propagator can achieve this, so any attempt to improvise on a windowsill would not be wholly successful.

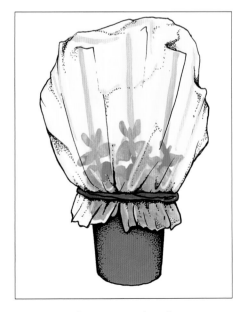

An improvised propagator where the plastic bag is supported by small sticks.

Seed sowing is a major part of propagation.

There are numerous plants, however, whose seed germinates readily without artificial warmth and will grow on without fuss. Many seeds can be sown directly into garden beds and this is often done to convey an air of natural placement in the display. It is risky in the sense that many seeds will be lost to pests and disease and, perversely, even success can be punished when seedlings are overcrowded and must be thinned out. Weeds will also germinate alongside and, even if they are correctly identified, their removal will usually disrupt the wanted seedlings. Probably, all seeds are better sown in pots or trays so that they can be properly positioned in the garden when they are sufficiently developed.

Those tender bedding plants and other subjects which would be damaged or killed by frost must be raised in the protected environment of the greenhouse, conservatory or inside windowsill. Small numbers can easily be grown in improvised conditions, especially if the varieties are chosen for their quick germination and robust constitution. As well as the savings in expenditure which can be made, there is a great deal of satisfaction to be gained.

At least a couple of catalogues list thousands of species for which seed is offered, and for the adventurous gardener the world's vegetation awaits exploration. Many of the plants listed will be unknown even to the experienced cultivators and will not be found in the normal retail catalogues. Seeds from trees and shrubs can cause problems for the amateur, usually in the long period which may be needed for germination but occasionally when the seeds need a period of chilling followed by a warm spell before they are aroused from dormancy. This sequence can be arranged by subjecting the seeds to a winter and spring outdoors or they can be placed in a freezer or refrigerator followed by a suitable temperature in a propagator.

Improvised systems can be very helpful but a heated propagator is an invaluable aid for raising seeds and cuttings. It provides controlled warmth and high humidity, which greatly improve a gardener's success rate. In winter it can be used as a protected environment for small, tender plants that might not survive in the home or cold greenhouse.

7 • CULTIVATION

Routine Cultivation

Watering

Even those doubting a strong commitment to gardening would be advised to consider the installation of an exterior tap which becomes immensely helpful if drought should occur. Water shortage is dramatic in its effect as significant losses can occur if rainfall is inadequate for a sustained period. Also, containers will always need regular watering even during normal summers. Struggling with a high indoor tap seems to be the norm but the convenience of outdoor access for watering cans and hoses is a great advantage.

Feeding

Feeding plants is only occasionally necessary, although it may be a more regular routine with culinary crops and those plants which are frequently pruned. Nonetheless, some plants face strong competition in the garden and if a lack of vitality is discernible, an appropriate measure of fertilizer can prove invaluable. If plants are decidedly lacklustre, it may be better to drench the foliage with a diluted liquid feed because this is more immediately usable by the plant. An annual dressing of a powdered or pelleted general fertilizer will benefit the whole garden if applied in the spring and will not prove to be expensive.

Mulching

Mulching is perhaps more important than chemical fertilizer because it conserves moisture in the soil, effectively suppresses annual weed growth and will play an important role in improving the soil texture. Peat was the traditional material for mulches but is now perhaps too expensive and its use has also attracted environmental criticism. Bark chippings make a longer-lasting mulch because they decompose slowly and hence their soil improvement

The plant enthusiast will find that most subjects can succeed in the confines of quite small pots but a nearby tap is essential for convenient watering.

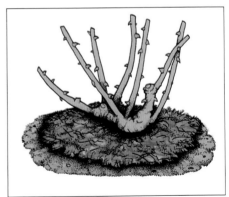

A mulch applied after weeding in the spring will conserve moisture, suppress further weeds and effect gradual soil improvement.

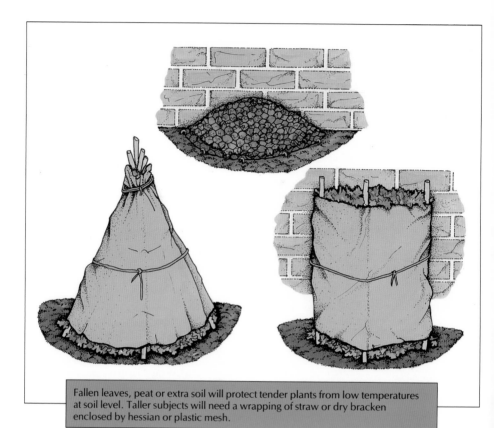

Fallen leaves, peat or extra soil will protect tender plants from low temperatures at soil level. Taller subjects will need a wrapping of straw or dry bracken enclosed by hessian or plastic mesh.

ability is also slower. The more economy-minded gardener will, if space permits, use a compost heap to recycle lawn cuttings and other garden waste into a home-made mulch which is as effective as any.

Maintenance

Weeds

These are usually common and indigenous plants which get a thoroughly bad press for being in the wrong place and arouse considerable antipathy. Except in totally neglected gardens, weeds are a very minor problem provided that treatment is carried out on a regular basis. Twenty minutes a week is much easier and more effective that one and a half hours each month due to the simple fact that small weeds are more easily removed or destroyed than large weeds. There are two basic methods for dealing with weed attack, one mechanical and the other chemical.

The hoe is the traditional weapon used against weeds but its record is not impressive. In clumsy hands or in crowded flowerbeds, it does not distinguish between friend and foe and much damage can result. When the soil is moist, the weed is dislodged by the hoe but is frequently left

The two main methods of weed control – chemical and mechanical. The finger and thumb has the least detrimental effect on the surrounding area and, when carried out regularly, is just as effective.

intact and able to re-root in a new position. The hoe is most effective in dry weather and in dry soil.

Least popular of the weeding methods is the finger and thumb which, properly deployed, will remove top growth and roots. It does involve some stooping or a hands-and-knees approach but this involves the useful by-product of allowing the gardener to come to close terms with the plants for detecting early problems or merely for appreciation of the low-level view. The smaller the weeds are when they are extracted, the easier the task is and the prospect of disturbing the other plants is reduced. The target system is to hand weed thoroughly in the spring and then apply a mulch of about 5cm (2in) depth. This will discourage the subsequent germination of weed seeds and any which do manage to

grow will be quickly identified and easily removed.

Weeds in paths and drives are most easily dealt with, although the narrowness of cracks and crevices makes digging them out rather difficult. A wide range of chemicals can be used including those which will kill all growth and these must be used with care to avoid them spreading into adjacent soil. Lawns seem to pose greater problems but there are selective weedkillers which kill plants with broad leaves and leave the narrow-leaved grasses unscathed. Those preferring not to use herbicides will be able to dig out large weeds like dandelions but clovers and daisies present much greater difficulty. Elsewhere in the garden when broad-leaved weeds mingle with prized plants, the selective weedkillers cannot be used wholesale, but where the infestation is moderate, the chemical solution can be applied to the weed leaves with a small paintbrush. In all situations, there are some extremely resilient weeds which may need a second application of herbicide before they are vanquished. Another immensely useful chemical weedkiller kills grasses while leaving broad-leaved plants untouched and comes into its own in tightly packed beds and rockeries which have been invaded by couch grass.

Pruning

The one permanent element of the garden is its ever-changing nature; not just from one season to another but because plants grow, develop, mature and compete with each other for light and space. Left to their own

Small scale pruning should be carried out regularly but when larger branches need removing, use the appropriate tool and take the necessary safety precautions.

devices, there would be winners and losers but in a managed situation, the gardener is the arbiter who must decide how much restraint or encouragement is needed. With trees and shrubs this will involve some surgical work which often arouses strong

feelings of trepidation. There is no real reason for apprehension because pruning is almost never fatal to the subjects. There is a tendency to wait until an intrusive branch becomes troublesome before reaching for the saw, whereas its earlier removal would not look so unsightly. Even so, there is little danger to the tree, even if large portions of it are cut away, as long as the proper precautions are taken to prevent the ingress of fungal growth.

The desirable approach is to treat pruning as an ongoing requirement and to make regular assessments of the woody subjects in the garden. Some anticipation of future growth will enable the identification of a small shoot which has the potential to grow into a badly placed branch, and the frequent removal of small amounts of growth will avoid the eyesores of wholesale pruning.

Herbaceous plants will also outgrow their allotted space and at some time it will be necessary to reduce the size of rampant plants. Early spring is the optimum time to dig out the whole plant, remove a healthy piece from the perimeter and replant it. The same principle applies to clusters of daffodils or other bulbs which may have become overgrown by virtue of their successful natural proliferation. The bulbs are readily detached from each other and a proportion can be replanted while the remainder can be offered to friends and neighbours or thrown away.

Undue encroachment is not the only reason for adjustments in the garden, for sometimes it will be occasioned by failure. Some plants, despite the initial care, may be in an unsuitable place and although they will rarely die quickly, they may just fade away. A desirable plant should be tried elsewhere in the garden and replaced by something more appropriate in the original position. The movement of plants can be overdone but nobody should think that planting is in any way final; transferred with

The laburnum is a lovely small tree with a graceful outline, distinctive foliage and long tassels of bright yellow flowers in the late spring. It will flower when quite small and young, and when mature, does not cast dense shade and rarely requires pruning. The leaves, twigs and especially the seeds are poisonous.

care and at the right time of the year, all plants can be transplanted successfully while they are fairly young and of manageable proportions.

A further reason for change is personal taste which will certainly alter during a gardening career. Different plants appeal at different times and since gardens clearly have a fixed occupancy rate, some exchanges are inevitable – when we fall in love with a new plant, an old one must go! Obviously, greater difficulties attend changes in trees and shrubs but smaller subjects in beds and rockeries can be changed frequently and without bother.

Even in gardens which depend on shrubs and perennials for the main displays, temporary plants should be considered for a seasonal change. The desirability of underplanting roses has been mentioned but many herbaceous borders have spaces which can be occupied by colourful annuals, and rockeries can be quite drab in summer unless short-term plants are introduced. Many of the smaller bedding plants are ideal, providing a continuance of interest without introducing strong competition for growing space.

Protection

The provision of protection for plants in the

Juniperus communis Compressa is a most useful dwarf conifer which will not exceed three feet when fully grown. The elegant, columnar shape and greyish green colouring enable it to blend easily in a variety of situations, including the rockery.

A greenhouse is an essential tool for keen gardeners.

garden is anathema to many gardeners who believe that the plants should be able to look after themselves. Some slightly tender subjects may be planted next to the house but to erect hessian or straw insulation for more exposed plants is beyond the pale. There is also a reluctance to provide stakes for taller plants because of the element of artificiality and the intrusive nature of some support systems. These are valid considerations for all gardeners but the distinction is between those who use a garden for purely ornamental purposes and those who are motivated to grow particular plants for the special pleasure that this can bring. A compromise position is possible if tender plants

are sited where shelter is naturally provided and taller specimens are supported in a totally discreet way.

Greenhouses and conservatories are protection systems which can be attractive features. Garden frames cannot be said to be attractive but they can be erected on a temporary basis from the onset of inclement weather. Rigid, transparent plastic is easily erected and quickly dismantled and stored, together with suitable fixing structures; this is a valuable option where garden space is at a premium. Otherwise, a permanent frame can be utilized throughout most of the year to protect susceptible crops.

8 • PESTS AND DISEASES

Pests

It is a comforting notion that small gardens have small pest problems and it is usually so! Actually, it has little to do with the size of the garden but much to do with the diversity of plants which are grown. Where an area contains a large concentration of similar or identical species, the risk of serious pestilence is always present but not where shrubs, trees, bulbs and different herbaceous plants make up the population.

There will be an abundance of insects but many of them are allies of the gardeners and should be cherished. The enemies may be legion but the problems that they cause are normally few and inconsequential. Greenfly, which are often brown and black as well, will always be found but they are an important source of food to other insects and small birds. Also known as aphids, they colonize young shoots and leaves to feed off the sap, and large numbers can deform or even kill fresh growth. Heavy rain washes them from the plants and this can be duplicated by using a forceful spray of water. An insecticide may be used if the infestation is severe or prolonged but environmentally aware gardeners will want to ensure that the chemical is only toxic to the target insects so that ladybirds and bees, for instance, are unharmed.

Whitefly is similarly widespread, especially on indoor plants, and may also require occasional treatment but serious infestations are unlikely in the garden. There are other creatures, such as caterpillars, which will inflict damage but action should be taken only if there is likely to be significant defoliation. Some gardeners prefer to take preventative measures by adopting a regular spray programme to eliminate pests but this will almost certainly lead to the death of many 'friendly' creatures.

The major menace in the home garden is undoubtedly the slug, which comes in various species of different shapes and

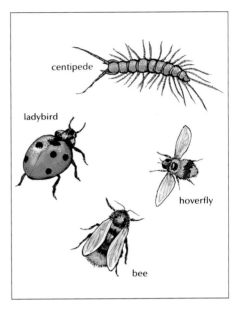

Random spraying can damage beneficial insects as well as destroy unwelcome ones.

colours but all have huge appetites for fresh plant growth. Herbaceous perennials and bedding plants are most at risk, particularly in the spring when they can be found climbing shrubs and house walls to reach the succulent new shoots. Considering their painfully slow pace and the vulnerability of the mollusc body, they are amazingly successful and have brought tears to the eyes of generations of gardeners. Anti-slug tactics have entered horticultural folklore but the application of cinders and use of beer-filled dishes have never been demonstrably effective.

A recent innovation involves the use of a liquid containing nematodes which invade the slug's body and bring about its death, but this treatment is still expensive. Slug pellets have low cost and proven efficiency to commend them but some gardeners are reluctant to distribute poisons where they

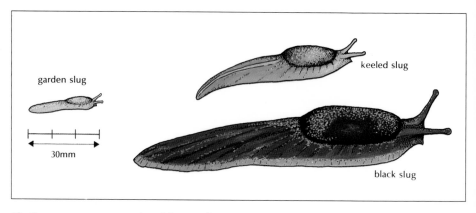

The three most common species of slugs are the major enemies of cultivated gardens, causing immense damage to soft, new growth.

are readily accessible. Pets and wild animals may be under slight threat from the pellets but the incidence of death or injury has not been widespread and those organizations which monitor the situation have not registered noticeable alarm. The manufacturers of slug pellets have sought to make them unpalatable to other creatures and seem to have been largely successful.

Many other members of the animal kingdom will gain sustenance from garden plants and could consequently be labelled as harmful but wholesale damage is unlikely except in country districts where rabbits and deer may get into gardens. Usually, cosmetic and superficial injury to plants will hardly be visible in the overall display and will rarely jeopardize the health of vegetation. If significant damage is noticed without the cause being known, it is advisable to seek advice so that suitable action can be taken.

Diseases

There are also hundreds, if not thousands, of micro-organisms which can have a harmful influence on plant life and they commonly take the form of a fungus which enters the plant tissue. Sometimes it can be a serious affliction and cultivators must be aware and vigilant especially during the growing season when moulds and mildew are most likely to occur. On a small scale, affected parts of a plant should be removed and the rest must be sprayed with a fungicide to inhibit the progress of disease. If the scale of infection is large or worrying, it is wise to seek advice from other gardeners, garden centres or from local parks staff.

The last few paragraphs have mentioned the use of fungicides, insecticides and herbicides which are chemically based. Please ensure that the written instructions are followed in the interests of garden safety.

GLOSSARY

Acid (soil)   Having a pH below 7.0.
Alkaline (soil)   Having a pH above 7.0.
Annual   A plant which completes its life cycle within one year.

Biennial   A plant which takes two years to complete its life cycle.
Bedding plant   A plant used for spring or summer flowering in beds.

Compost   A mixture of loam, sand and other ingredients which is used to grow plants in pots. Also means decayed vegetation produced on a compost heap.
Cultivar   A cultivated variety of plant not produced in the wild.

Deciduous   Plants which lose their leaves in winter.
Dormant   When a plant stops growing, usually in winter.

Evergreen   Plants which bear foliage throughout the year.

Fungicide   Chemical which kills fungi.

Geometric   Made up of simple shapes such as circles, triangles, rectangles.

Half-hardy   A plant which is usually killed by frost.

Hardy   A plant which is resistant to temperatures around freezing.
Herbaceous   Soft plants which do not form a persistent woody stem.
Herbicide   Chemical which kills vegetation, sometimes selectively.

Indigenous (plants)   Wild, native plants.
Insecticide   Chemical which kills insects, sometimes selectively.

Landscaping   The arrangement of plants and other features together.

Microclimate   The climate which prevails in the garden or part thereof.
Mulch   Layer of compost or other material spread over the soil.

Peat   Partly decomposed vegetation used in composts and to improve soils.
Perennial   A plant which has a life-span of more than two years.
Pergola   A timber or metal framework designed as a walkway and plant support.
pH   The measurement scale of acidity and alkalinity between 1 and 14.
Propagation   The reproduction of plants by means of seeds, cuttings, etc.

Trellis   A light framework of wood or plastic for supporting plants.

INDEX